Red State, Blue State

Black Hamlet

Dedication

This book is dedicated to a future where intelligence, effort and the drive to leave the world a little better for our passing are celebrated, honored and lauded as examples worthy of following.

By contrast, this future precludes the narratives of greed, ignorance and hate, placing them firmly in the "unevolved" and "lessons learned" categories.

Self awareness requires sacrifice – global awareness requires even more. Sometimes bravery is standing unarmed before an avalanche of guns. Sometimes bravery is pulling the trigger. Wisdom is understanding the difference.

Black Hamlet 2017

Foreword

This book is a collection of form and free verse poetry, all of which was written specifically for this book.

'Red State, Blue State' is an American-centric treatment of what has become a global problem: the death rattle of anachronistic, misogynistic, bigoted and xenophobic points of view, supported by specious and bile-inducing rhetoric.

As a species we are greater than the sum of our parts, but only when we set the conditions to allow individuality to enhance society as a whole, not break it down into component pieces for easier consumption.

Black Hamlet 2017

Table of Contents

Two ears

So many diverse arguments, for years,
Two sides with polar opposite beliefs;
The difference between the two, two ears.

Opinions grounded in disparate fears,
Where animosity precludes relief;
So many diverse arguments, for years,

That in the end it's only us we hear.
Two sides of the same coin that rarely speak,
The difference between the two, two ears.

We doubt, mistrust, engage hate over beer
That's brewed with just the right amount of grief;
So many diverse arguments, for years,

That now there is no forest, only trees.
When did we sell our reasoning to thieves
Whose only major difference, two ears?

We sow our conflicts, reaping only tears
Which bleach our lives like unattended reefs;
So many diverse arguments, for years,
The difference between the two, two ears.

Your condescension

Your condescension irks me to the bone,
How dare you tell us all how we must live?
Fly over us to make your way back home?
As meaningless as what you say you give.

Sure, we still live within communities,
And fear the God who ravages the land;
Confusing faith with rank stupidity
You slide your eyeballs down your nose and stand

Upon the backs of those who farm and feed
With arrogance you never even earned.
What makes you think you understand our needs?
What makes you think you have the right to burn

Our flag, our rights, our way of life, our love,
Because you think you do not have enough?

The world's moved on

The world's moved on from Bhagat Singh and Klan,
We do not live in 1923;
You say you are a *real* American
But all we see is hate and bigotry.

We heard you whisper "nigger in the House,"
And proudly state you'd pray the gay away;
When we envision futures that are ours
We see one where you morons don't hold sway.

It's guns and NRA and vengeful gods,
And Liberals destroying all that's good
Each time we wander into Red State sods
Who mouth the words as if they're understood.

You want to be Pro Life well here's a hint:
Turn those guns upon yourselves and finish it.

Immigration

Don't say there are no jobs, invite them in
and give them chances we don't ever see;
it's only lawyers making cash money
on every Perez, Huang, Petrov and Kim.
We welcome those who integrate, come in
without their burkas, turbans and their beads;
they're visitors and we think that their needs
should coincide with ours – is that a sin?

Those Mosques might not mean much on either coast,
but here they perpetrate mistrust and fear;
these symbols of invasion like a boast
that they can do just what they want once here.
What happened to our sov'reign rights as hosts?
What happened to our proud Democracy?

No, immigration

Prioritized enforcement, not a ban,
we wish to embrace all who grace our shores;
we sell our dream, they come for wanting more
than slavery, dictatorship, bombed vans.
We share ideas and cultures where we can,
inclusive-democratic with our laws;
we welcome the downtrodden and the poor
as humans first, not pawns in partisan

demands, all lobbied for with corp'rate cash.
Our graciousness speaks louder than our fears,
where bigotry just fills our mouths with ash;
our dreams not meant to fill a life with tears
nor recreate a past lie where we bash
the easy targets for our lazy years.

Freedom

Life, liberty and freedom all remain
The cornerstone of our Democracy;
So, order and tradition we maintain
To save our country from insanity.

Political correctness damned us all,
No God in these decisions, so we fall
Below the standards we all need for Grace,
Back-pedaling Left until we have no face.

You don't know what freedom is

The Bill of Rights protects amendments – ten
To be exact, for greater liberties
And limiting the power of Government
So we can live with some civility.

To bigotry, stupidity and hate
There's no support in law, and no mandate;
You think you are a lion when you roar
But all you are, my friends, are dinosaurs.

The Yin & Yang of Centrists

The center
always badly compromised,
surprised to find itself as useful
as a bull with tits,
or Trump's kids in the West Wing where
all care for themselves
but no responsibility.

The media
hates centrists most of all;
extremes provide good copy and
sound bits sound much better shouted
than delivered evenly,
like toothpaste.

With first amendment specificity
the coverage of a fact remains
a stain upon democracy,
intelligence,
by virtue of a bias
still maintained
by sponsors and the folks
who pay the bills.

Let's kill the media,
bring back the News.

Your (D)

You think that "D" means you can criticize
Americans who aren't as smug as you,
demeaning us with lawyer-speak and lies
to gain support with National Network News.

You think this country three States, maybe four,
where atheists and deviants hold sway;
but our boys are the ones who go to war
to let you whining pussies have your say.

We work a day before you're out of bed,
our labor in the fields and mines is tough;
we work to make sure all of you are fed
but you say what we do is not enough.

No wonder we cling firmly to our guns,
the battle for America's begun.

Your (R)

You think the "R" initialed with your name
means that you own God and patriots;
a "D" or "I" is really not the same,
pretending to be something that they're not,

Like RINO's or those centrists you despise.
You think all non-conservatives are dupes
who really need to open up their eyes;
you *know* you are the owners of the *Truth*

Coz Fox and Friends says that's the way it is,
And Breitbart, Rush and money all agree.
You see yourselves as Valjean from Les Mis,
hard done by and repressed, but now you're free.

How come your lobbyists are billionaires?
Why do you fight each bill for cleaner air?

What is small Government?

Republicans have championed smaller size,
and sold it as a non-intrusive means
for Government to let us live our lives
without those regulations which demean.

But what they mean is much less oversight,
(think EPA and FEC with Trump);
 they packaged greed and sold it as a right,
a semi with no brakes and no speed bumps.

Then Democrats shout "we can't trust these men!
We'll make more jobs to suckle at the teat
of taxes we control, so now and then
we find a loophole through which we can sneak.

Corruption always is bi-partisan,
don't shoot a fact exposed by either side;
but please, by God, learn everything you can
so you won't victimize yourself with lies.

I am

I am the Pro Life, market-driven God
whose carbon footprint my true to gift to you;
the creatures of the plains and seas are yours
to hunt and kill and eat and mount on walls.

I am the Pro Choice, regulated God
who has a say in everything you do;
I don't expect your worship, and my cause
requires the rich to help pay for the poor.

I am the NATO, anti-Russian God
who sanctions every layer just for you;
my brother is a Muslim who abhors
restrictions unless they are Islam's Laws.

I am the man who wakes up every morning
to hear you argue about global warming
as if fact somehow a conspiracy,
as if the planet does not affect me.

I am the man who says there is no God,
just decency, humanity, and death;
your arguments disgust me to the point
where I'll not draw another zealot breath.

The Democrat heifer

My farm has a Democrat heifer
Who's stylish and quite a nice dresser;
Got her hoofs stuck in mud,
Said "Oh boy, now I'm fucked,"
Farmer said, "not now and not ever!"

A reporter from far CNN
Took a liking to heifer and when
Nobody was looking
Stuck both of his hands in,
Said, "I'm vegan, but beef now and then."

He left and my cattle were pregnant,
Who knew less than one inch, a segment,
Could fill up their bellies
With twelve piebald nellies
All born with no milk ducts, and no sense?

I would sell them to fast food concerns
But one thing, as a farmer, I've learned
Is that folks won't eat meat
When it has human feet
An can't walk without taking left turns.

Republican science

I studied Republican science,
Alternative facts with Right bias;
We prayed away gayness,
Not knowing what that is
Until my instructors compliant.

I learned all about Global Warming,
And how it was Chinese performing
An act to reduce us
And make us quite useless
In this New World Order we're forming.

They explained that the world really flat,
And the only real problem with that
Was that Rush Limbaugh's chair
Would just slide everywhere
If we listened to Democrat "facts."

We learned how all migrants are Muslims
Who landed here all of a sudden;
I went up to Utah
Coz that's where my folks are,
And promptly remarried my cousin.

We need

We need good jobs, and better schools, and wages!
We don't want Wall Street sellout crap corruption!
We don't want Government to build us cages!

We need a healthcare system that's not broken,
And real oversight that is not partisan;
We want to live without your interruption

That's delivered by another charlatan.
"Too Left! Too Right!" Extremist is the label
That's used by every woman, child and boy-man,

Although the center very overcrowded
With those from both sides of the civic table.
Our foreheads flat from speciousness that's pounded

Into us to justify the argument
That corp'rate cash must ratify the Government.

The threat

The existential threat from those extremists,
A tidal wave, illegal immigration;

 A government completely out of touch
With existential threats from those extremists.

Planned Parenthood, the Common Core – economy?
Look! Existential threats from those extremists!

The regulations have to go, like honey bees
Who sting with existential threats – extremists!

We have to arm ourselves, a call to arms!
Against the existential threat – ourselves.

Another kind of threat

My babies cry, I give them what they want,
We need to give them everything they want.

We separate the lives that matter most,
We need to give them everything they want.

Black lives, Brown lives, Poor lives, immigrants,
We need to give them everything they want.

Uneducated, isolationist,
We need to give them everything they want.

Those interests that align with ours – donations,
We need to give them everything they want.

We gave them what they asked for, drained us dry,
Now we don't have a friggin' thing they want!

Gun rights position

Interpretation of the Second says,
The right to bear arms, part of Liberty;
No partial ban, restrictions, should we see
By referencing the First, extended "Press."

Like oil that ships from ports in cold Valdez
The arguments are fluid, guns v "we;"
Interpretation of the Second says,
The right to bear arms, part of Liberty.

You can't predict the numbers, more or less,
Of those intent on killing or to steal;
The value of your castle, family,
Determines assault rifles sometimes best,
Interpretation of the Second says.

Gun control position

Militia, regulated, not one man,
Guns threaten general welfare, should be banned
Unless in strict defense of life and land.
Mass shootings, suicide, not healthy plans.

No proof that Liberty strained by a ban,
Regardless of the rhetoric that's fanned
By NRA and Senators who ran
On tickets funded by gun maker's hands.

The psychos escalate because they can,
Weak background checks boost sales – it seems so
planned;
Do nothing and our country will be damned
By victims cut down well before their span.
Militia, regulated, not one man.

Some impeach cobbler, humble pie

In Yermo, California,
my favorite spot is Peggy Sues;
old fashioned burgers, curly fries,
a dozen different pies to choose.

Columbus Circle, Central Park,
Per Se; slightly different dining
just a few blocks from the Hudson,
Carnegie Hall, the Kitchen too.

TownHall in Ohio, Canoe
in Georgia, Chattahoochee way;
no matter where you eat these days
everybody wants their say.

Conservative and Liberal,
though enemies, cannot deny,
the President's Executive
needs impeach cobbler, humble pie.

My dairy farm

I'm up at 4am, black coffee, toast.
It's bike or horse to herd the cows to shed,
to join the team, check out the stock, and dote
on those new sick or lame, to call the vet.

Hose down the milking shed then breakfast time.
Today it's fencing, tractor and the weeds,
tomorrow, seeds, and mountains I must climb
to try and find that yearling, disappeared.

Lunch and chores and milking once again,
then paperwork and ordering, fixing
things I should have done last week back when
I swear it was much quieter before Spring.

I wonder if those lib'ral hacks back East
could handle five long minutes with these beasts?

My trading desk

From Flushing, Queens, The Bronx, up to the Street
by Hooptie, Whip or Subway, all the same;
an hour lost to early morning heat
to make my 7am call, my name.

Structured assets, longer hours, and models,
roll out 8pm and client drinks;
she's too rachet, already I can tell
she prolly blows real well but never thinks.

Work Sundays, public holidays, late nights,
2 bed, 1 bath, Tribeca, just 10 G's;
for 3 or 4k clean, but out of sight,
welcome to the city of New York, na'mean?

I wonder if those nut jobs in the sticks
know just how tough it is to work with pricks?

Northern Ireland

The century had ended, Northern Ireland,
And still the Troubles fresh in people's thinking;
Was there to witness Bobby take Siobhan's hand,

Mixed marriage, Prot and Catholic, mud slinging
Part and parcel of the celebratory day,
And it got worse as people started drinking.

Now some sixteen years have passed, I moved away
To live in these United States, a migrant
From a country where we "hang shit" every day,

And tolerate most everything but tyrants.
I'm here to tell you bluntly I've not seen worse.
They say shit flows downhill and gets more fragrant,

Which must explain how each State here is cursed
With legislation written by Trump's Turds.

BTFO

BTFO, you libtard cuck!
Where's your Safe Space now, you PC loon?
Regressive Left, no safety net
for Snowflakes, little Buttercups.

Those imgrants don't speak English, take our jobs,
And fuck Islam! And Hillary too!
And fuck the Dark State
all controlled by aliens!

Clinton News Network, CNN,
and those elitist pricks on NBC;
let's run the country like a bizness,
make America great again!

I don't believe the shit I hear,
it's Fake News and the Media!
That Russian stuff, a lie, I know,
Coz trump says that it is.

Basement dweller

Basement Dweller, Birther – Drumpf!
Conspiritard, Deplorable!
Trumpkin with your Velcro Shoes,
anyone you raped today?

Misogynistic, racist piece of shit,
you climbed back in the ooze today
reversing Darwin's theory
for all time.

When fake Global Warming
floods your home and business
how many rounds will you let loose
to prove you're tougher than the earth?

We no longer see the need
to improve background check legislation
to weed out the insane and mentally ill -
it seems we are already way too late.

Enough

The hurricanes and floods are not enough?
The senseless inner-city deaths, the Left,
The Right, and neither of them really tough.
The only thing they're good at is mass theft.

Remember when you held your flag with pride?
And those that didn't, welcomed on the ride
To welcome the downtrodden and the poor
To these United States, these golden shores.

When did the Dream become so partisan?
When did we come to fear the world so much?
We've crippled every candidate who ran
Until our politicians out of touch.

They say that once you know you can't go back,
America much bigger than that fact;
We sing that we're the Brave and we're the Free,
Let's make it real and take back Liberty!

Speaking truth to conspiracy

Sean Hannity, Ann Coulter, Rush Limbaugh,
of course they know more than the CIA;
they're patriots who understand the "how,"
explain it to us in their simple way.

Poor Mary Lou Bruner was targeted
by Facebook hackers looking to pollute
the truth of why the dinosaurs all dead,
the fact Obama was a prostitute.

While we're on Obama … secret Muslim,
a Kenyan sneaking in Sharia law;
Obamacare "Death panels" and the sin
of immigrants just flooding 'cross the wall.

The only thing that stopped these evil plans
was honest Christian folk – Republicans.

Active measures

Travel ban, trail balloon for coup d'état,
plot to control our universities;
then demonize opinions from the Right
because they hate, can't stand the Hillary.

The minute that we play, we're being played,
how can we criticize when we're like this?
All active measures work when they're relayed,
regardless of intentions – palms or fists.

Legitimize a circus, suffer clowns,
and Networks know what people pay to see;
you cannot dress hyperbole in gowns
then claim you have superiority.

Our downfall is our hubris and disdain,
we never recognized our peoples' pain.

Where is the world?

Where is the world I use to know,
Of simple things and Sunday meals?
Where is my past, where did it go,
Where is the world I use to know?
Where are the seeds I used to sow?
Where are the loves I used to feel?
Where is the world I use to know,
Of simple things and Sunday meals?

How did we get to this?

The past a barren, trampled field
Of dark and deep-set memories;
Don't ask me how it is I feel,
The past a barren, trampled field.
The future only what I steal
From apple pie based treacheries,
The past a barren, trampled field
Of dark and deep-set memories.

Responsibility

You stand upon the podium and mouth
All care and no responsibility;
No matter whispered words or deaf'ning shouts,
These are the actions to the words we hear.

All care and no responsibility,
As if you only want us for our vote;
These are the actions to the words we hear,
Your lies deny those messages of hope.

As if you only want us for our vote,
You speak to us as numbers, not as men;
Your lies deny those messages of hope,
Confusing graft with business acumen.

You speak to us as numbers, not as men,
A pool to save those drowning on the coast;
Confusing graft with business acumen,
You leave our town to scurry home and boast.

A pool to save those drowning on the coast,
No matter whispered words or deaf'ning shouts,
You leave our town to scurry home and boast -
You stand upon the podium and mouth …

Transparency

You slip onto the stage so quietly,
With words so colored by your checkered past
It's hard to swallow as you piously
Regale us with some levity, for laughs.

With words so colored by your checkered past
Not one man here inclined to cut you slack;
Regale us with some levity, for laughs,
But that won't take our cynicism back.

Not one man here inclined to cut you slack,
Nor take you at the value of your face;
Politeness holds our cynicism back
As you explain the reasons for disgrace.

We'll take you at the value of your face
When Hellfire freezes like the deep Midwest;
As you explain the reasons for disgrace,
We steer the course that we consider best.

When Hellfire freezes like the deep Midwest
We'll listen to your improprieties,
And steer the course that we consider best
As you slip off the stage so quietly.

Daddy, tell me

"Please, daddy, tell me, what's America?"
"Well, my child, it happened long ago,
to people who were once like you and me;
who lived near calm blue oceans and had snow,
abundance and good government,
clean water, food, and tolerance,
a place where all the world
wanted to go."

"That sounds a lot like fairy tales to me."

"It was a land of zealotry,
but coupled with community
and the firm belief
that anything was possible."

"Where are they now?
Where did they go?
And daddy, tell me,
is it true that they had snow?"

"What's left of what was once the greatest land
is hidden behind massive walls
nine thousand miles in length, and two miles high.
It's only visible from way up high.

And space."

"It doesn't sound
that great a place
to me."

"For decades it was envied for its wealth,
and fire power, military,
high living standard
where the people free.
And though they fought off
many enemies,
no-one could save them
when they fought themselves."

"Why would they harm themselves, it makes no
sense?"

"The fence was only part of it,
it seems some leaders got so desperate
they made up lies, insisted they were truths.
And proof became so partisan
that every woman, child and man
was forced to choose a side."

"Is that what made them harm themselves?"

"No, my sweet young child.
In the end,

that is the thing
that made them turn upon themselves
and die."

"Not one of them survived?"

"I hope not, my sweet love,
I truly do."

www.ingramcontent.com/pod-product-compliance
Lightning Source LLC
Chambersburg PA
CBHW050848290526

45792CB00002B/576